History of Entertainment

Jack Harvey

Macdonald Educational

Contents

How to use this book
Look first at the contents page and see if the subject you are looking for is listed. For instance if you want to find out about orchestras, you will see that The Orchestra is on page 22. The index will tell you where and how many times a particular subject is listed. For instance you will see that violin is listed on pages 9 and 22.

What is Entertainment?

Entertainment has probably existed since people first appeared on the Earth. The way people enjoy themselves has changed with the different forms of civilisation. This book looks at different kinds of entertainment and shows some of the things people do when they want to enjoy themselves.

People who work too hard and never relax soon become ill. Entertainment helps us to relax and stay healthy. When we are performing for other people, or watching our favourite show as spectators, we feel happy and excited. Entertainment can give us something to think about and something to look forward to.

In the early days of history people enjoyed themselves in simple ways. They told stories, played sports, sang, danced and made music. Nowadays we enjoy different forms of the same entertainment. We go to discotheques and music concerts. We watch exciting stories on television. We still enjoy competition and sport.

Mediaeval minstrels used to sing and tell stories about the brave deeds of knights

The Story-teller

A good story has always been one of the most popular forms of entertainment. Before there were any books stories had to be told out loud. At first people used to meet at night and talk about the day's events. They told one another where to hunt the best animals and which wild foods were good to eat. This information was more important to them than the television news is to us. Often there was news about a war. A good story-teller invented details of his own to make the battles more exciting. Listeners enjoyed a good story so much that no-one minded if it was not all true.

Each country had its own stories about the great soldiers of the past and the gods who protected them. The legends of Greece were very exciting. Homer wrote them down 3,000 years ago. A famous story was about the Greeks going to war against the city of Troy.

In parts of Africa and India story-tellers are still very important. Stories are just as popular today in Britain. That is why films like 'Jaws' and television serials like 'Starsky and Hutch' and 'Coronation Street' are so successful.

Millions enjoy the story of 'Coronation Street' on television

All the family listens to
the old story-teller's tales

For the fans a football
match is one of the best
kinds of entertainment

Music and Dance

When people are very happy they often jump up and down. They may also clap their hands and shout. Fans at pop concerts and festivals scream and wave their arms when they see their favourite group. People who are upset also sometimes wave their arms in the air. They walk about restlessly and moan. Music and dance have their roots in the way people react to strong feelings of all kinds.

All over the world there are rain dances, harvest dances and dances to celebrate births and marriages.

In the Austrian Tirol there is a dance called the Schuhplattler (shoe sole dance). Like many folk dances it tells a story. A man is trying to attract a girl. He slaps his thighs, knees and heels and stamps his feet to the rhythm of the music. Then he leaps in the air and turns cartwheels. Lastly he lifts the girl up and swings her around his body.

Nowadays this dance is performed to entertain tourists. But once it was part of a spring festival. People sang and danced as a way of praying to their gods. In return they believed the gods would give them good crops and healthy livestock. Many folk dances began as these fertility dances or as religious rituals.

Modern Dancing

Many people find dancing one of the best ways of relaxing. On Friday or Saturday night they go to meet friends at clubs, dance halls and discotheques.

The Flamenco dances of Spain began as fertility dances

A Scottish dancer. Every country has its own dances

Fans enjoy a pop festival

Early Musical Instruments

The earliest instruments were made from very simple materials. People found that they could make interesting sounds by knocking bones or sticks together. They stretched an animal's skin tight over the hollow section of a tree trunk and made a drum. They made a trumpet from a cow's horn. The first flute was a hollow reed or cane and holes drilled along its length made it possible to play different notes and make a tune.

The first stringed instrument was made from animal gut tied across a bent piece of wood. Different thicknesses of gut gave different sounds.

The violin is only one modern instrument which has taken thousands of years to develop. Its earliest ancestors were single-stringed lutes from places as far apart as Egypt and Ireland. Gradually through the centuries different musicians added strings and altered the shape until it developed into its present form.

Simple discoveries such as these led the way to all the instruments of the modern orchestra and rock group.

Arabian Rebab

Gaelic Crouth

Viol

Violin

North American Indians perform a ritual dance in the snow

The violin is 300 years old. Before it there were other kinds of stringed instruments

Comedy and Cruelty

The world is a dangerous place. Earthquakes, fires, floods and hurricanes can destroy cities overnight. Wars and the threat of wars are everyday events. Even in peacetime thousands die every day in road accidents. Films and television plays show similar violence. Westerns, detective thrillers and films like 'Towering Inferno' prove that audiences are both afraid of danger and fascinated by it.

People often laugh at scenes in shows which would be very serious if they happened in real life. Circus clowns pretend to be cruel. They hit one another over the head and make fools of each other. Their surprise and anger make us laugh. But they are only funny because we know that no-one is really being hurt.

When film comedians like Laurel and Hardy balance on the edge of a building the audience laughs because it knows the film will end happily.

Violence Past and Present

The gladiator shows of ancient Rome were very violent. 50,000 spectators watched them fight in the arena of the Colosseum. When a gladiator fell, a thumbs down sign from the Emperor condemned him to death. Sometimes the arena was flooded and battles were fought from ships. The crowd also saw Christians being torn to pieces by wild animals.

The modern bullfight also takes place in an arena. Crowds come to watch and applaud the contest between the bullfighter (matador) and the bull.

Many people feel that modern entertainment is too violent. This may be so, but violence and cruelty have long been a part of entertainment.

Laurel and Hardy are afraid they are going to fall off this high building. We laugh at their terror because we know they will escape

Cockfighting was once very popular with gamblers. They put their money on a bird and then watched to see which cock would be killed

Fairs and Festivals

At the fair nothing seems real. There is loud music. Coloured lights flash and there is gaudy paintwork everywhere. Fast-talking 'barkers' tempt us to spend money on a space-ship ride or at a bingo stall. Passengers shriek as they spin on the Ferris wheel or collide on dodgems. Fairs travel round the country. All the rides and sideshows are unpacked from trucks and set up in parks. After a week or two they move to the next town.

How Fairs Began

Fairs began as markets. Merchants went twice a year to Troyes in France, to buy and sell goods. In England the largest fair was at Stourbridge, near Cambridge. Jugglers, tight-rope walkers and fortune-tellers followed the crowds. In the end the entertainment became more important than the trading.

The Rides

The earliest roundabouts were small. They had to be turned by hand. Big roundabouts and the giant Ferris wheel were invented in the 19th century. Then they were powered by steam. Now diesel motors are used.

Pleasure Gardens

In the 18th and 19th centuries there were permanent fairs called Pleasure Gardens. In London at Vauxhall there were firework displays, concerts and battles between knights in mediaeval armour. The Prater in Vienna and the Tivoli in Copenhagen are two old pleasure gardens which still exist.

Carnivals and Festivals

Christians often have big celebrations at the start of Lent. They are called carnivals. In mediaeval Florence there

Holi is the Hindu Spring Festival. Everyone dances in the streets

People enjoy being thrown around by the fairground 'rides'

were processions. Huge gilded palaces were built on carts. Giants walked beside them on stilts. And there were battles between people dressed as angels and devils. In Nice the carnival still ends with a battle of flowers. In New Orleans Shrove Tuesday has the old French name of 'Mardi Gras'. Everyone wears fancy dress. They dance and sing in the streets. The carnivals of Trinidad are just as merry.

The Chinese celebrate their New Year in much the same way. People dress up as dragons and run through the streets. They let off firecrackers to frighten away evil spirits.

The Hindu Spring Festival is called Holi. Coloured water is sprayed around during the processions. Red powder is thrown over the spectators. There is loud music on drums and horns.

All these festivals began as holy days. Today they are mainly a chance for people to have fun together.

Fairs are full of noise and colour

The 'Galloper' is a traditional ride

The Circus

The circus comes to most big towns at least once a year. Children are taken to see it as a treat. It is difficult to tell who enjoys it most, the parents or the children. Circus shows have clowns, acrobats and performing animals. Big circuses go on tour to many different countries and continents.

Animal Acts

Only female elephants are used in circuses. They are easier to tame than the males. There has to be complete trust between the trainer and the animals. This trust can be shown when the trainer lies on his back. He lets the elephant lower its foot to within a few centimetres of his face. He lies very still. A sudden noise or movement could frighten the animal into crushing him.

Acrobats and Bareback Riders

Most circus stars come from circus families. They have to start training when they are very young. Ella Bradna was a great acrobat on horseback. It was many years before she could dance on the back of a racing horse or turn somersaults as she leapt from one horse to another.

Clowns

There are many different circus clowns. Often circus clowns come into the ring in groups and play tricks on each other. Each clown has his own character and funny way of dressing.

The original clown has a white face and hides his hair under a white stocking cap. He wears a spangled suit and flat slippers. Another kind of clown is called Auguste. His suit is baggy and his wig very untidy. He trips over his huge clumsy shoes.

The flame-thrower throws flaming knives at his partner

Performing tigers are one of the most popular acts

Music Halls and Musicals

Variety shows are very popular on television. Comedians, singers, magicians and ventriloquists all take part. This kind of show could be seen 100 years ago in a music hall. People went to the music halls to eat and drink as well as to hear the popular songs of the day.

People enjoyed the comedy of music halls. When a comedian came on stage and made jokes the audience often shouted back.

The Stars

Marie Lloyd who was born in 1870 was a great star of London's music halls. She came from the same poor background as most of her audience. She was cheeky and helped them to laugh at their troubles. Her song 'Don't Dilly Dally on the Way' is about a family who cannot afford to pay the rent.

The Scots singer Harry Lauder was born in 1870, the same year as Marie Lloyd. He sang serious songs like 'Keep Right on to the End of the Road' and comic songs as well. He began as a coal-miner. In the end he earned as much as £1,000 a week.

Variety Theatres Today

The cinema and later, television, put an end to most variety theatres. But there are still some live variety shows. There are variety shows at many large seaside towns. At working men's clubs in Britain people eat and drink while they watch the show, just as they did in the music halls.

The London Palladium is a famous variety theatre in England.

Charlie Chaplin

Harry Lauder

Marie Lloyd

Sammy Davis Junior

Vaudeville and Hollywood

Most of the comedians in early films began in vaudeville, the American name for variety. W. C. Fields did a comic act as a drunken billiard player. Buster Keaton did an act with his parents when he was a tiny child.

Several British comedians went to America to try their luck in films. Charlie Chaplin and Stan Laurel of Laurel and Hardy are two such famous stars.

The First Musicals

A musical is a play with songs and dances as well as spoken scenes. Light opera became popular in the 19th century. Operas like 'Orpheus in the Underworld' by Offenbach and 'The Mikado' by Gilbert and Sullivan all have good tunes and the latter pokes fun at pompous people. These were really early musicals.

Broadway Hits

Many famous musicals were first performed on Broadway. Broadway is a street in New York which is famous for its theatres. Richard Rodgers composed songs for more than 40 Broadway musicals. The best known are 'Oklahoma' and 'The Sound of Music'. Both have words by Oscar Hammerstein and were filmed. In the 1970's Rock Musicals like 'Hair' and 'Jesus Christ Superstar' have had great success.

Musicals on Stage and Screen

Many great variety stars have also acted in stage and screen musicals. Ethel Merman was for 25 years Broadway's top star. 'Annie Get Your Gun' was written for her. Sammy Davis Jr played in 'Mr Wonderful' on Broadway and in the film of 'Sweet Charity'. But he is more famous for his solo acts at places like the London Palladium.

17

Early Theatre

Nowadays there are plays and films every night on television. But there are still theatres in most cities where actors perform plays to a 'live' audience. Being part of an audience at a play is like being at a football match. Everyone shares the excitement.

Theatre began more than 2,500 years ago in Greece. People sang and danced in the open air to celebrate great occasions and religious festivals.

At these festivals, a chorus of men sang and told stories about gods and heroes. In Greek plays it was easy for the same actors to play many parts because they wore masks. The mask showed what kind of person the actor was playing. Even the female parts were played by men. Women were not allowed to act.

Mystery Plays

During the Middle Ages people watched plays about the Christian religion. These early plays were acted on carts in the street. They were called mystery plays, because each scene was acted by workers from one of the trades or 'mysteria'.

The first simple plays were about the birth and death of Jesus. Later plays were

Epidaurus, an ancient Greek theatre, seated 12,000 people

The first actors wore masks

Throughout the Middle Ages religious festivals such as Corpus Christi were celebrated by mystery plays which were acted on carts in the streets. All the stories were from the Bible

more realistic. They were sometimes about men being killed because they would not give up their religion.

Shakespeare and the Globe

In the 16th century people began to build open-air theatres in large towns.

William Shakespeare (1564–1616) is Britain's most famous playwright. Most of his plays like 'Hamlet' and 'Macbeth' were acted at the Globe Theatre in London. There was no scenery. But he could make people believe that the actors were in a forest, on a beach or in a castle, just by the words he used. There were still no actresses. Romeo's Juliet and Lady Macbeth were first played by teenage boys.

Shakespeare's Globe

This is how a cross-section of Shakespeare's Globe Theatre may have looked. Most of the audience stood in the yard to watch the play. They were known to Shakespeare as the 'groundlings'. Richer people paid more to sit under cover in the galleries. The roof of the stage was painted to look like the sky. But there was no scenery and very few pieces of furniture in the Globe plays. The balconies at the back of the stage were permanent and used in many plays. Behind them were the dressing rooms where the actors put on their costumes. A flag was flown when the play was about to start. Circular theatres like these were also used for bull and bear baiting

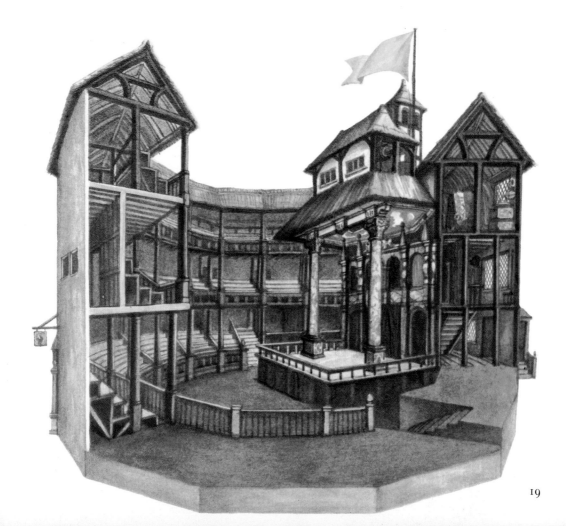

Indoor Theatre

The first indoor theatres were rooms in private houses. But the Olympic at Vicenza, in Northern Italy, was built as a theatre. It opened in 1584 and is still in use.

Louis XIV started the Comédie Française in Paris in 1680. The company still exists. By this time women were beginning to act in all European theatres.

In the 18th and 19th century theatres got larger and more richly decorated. Walls were painted and carved. The seats were covered with velvet.

On stage there was spectacular scenery. Complicated machines made it possible to have on stage what looked like live horse races and ship wrecks.

Nowadays many people prefer very simple theatres, like Chichester Theatre which is in England. It is very bare. There is no curtain and scenery is changed in full view of the audience. Many theatre companies now like to get the audience more involved with what is happening on stage.

Sarah Bernhardt (1844-1923) was the most famous French actress of the 19th century

Putting on a Play

A large team of people is needed to put on a play. The playwright writes the script. The actors learn the lines and 'moves'. The director guides them as to how they should act. Technicians work the lights and tape-recorders for the important 'noises-off', such as a pistol shot or a cheering crowd. A wardrobe mistress looks after the costumes. There also have to be people to sell tickets, programmes and drinks.

Learning to Act

A drama school course may last three years. Students also learn to fence and dance. They have lessons in speech and singing. In mime classes they try to express feelings without using any words. They also learn to improvise by making up a play without a script.

Acting in Public Places

Actors often work in pubs, factories and schools as well as in theatres and even in the street as in the Middle Ages. Sometimes they ask the audience to join in the action of the play. By putting on plays in these places actors can choose their audience rather than the other way round.

A good actor can take on a wide variety of tragic or comic roles: the famous actor Laurence Olivier

The Chichester Festival Theatre is neat and plain. It has an 'open' stage, like many modern theatres. No curtain hides the stage before the start of the show. The audience watches from three sides of the stage

These plans show how a 'proscenium stage' theatre works. Scenery is changed by 'flying' it up into the fly tower. Furniture can be stored in the wings, which are the areas on either side of the stage. The green room is where actors wait between scenes

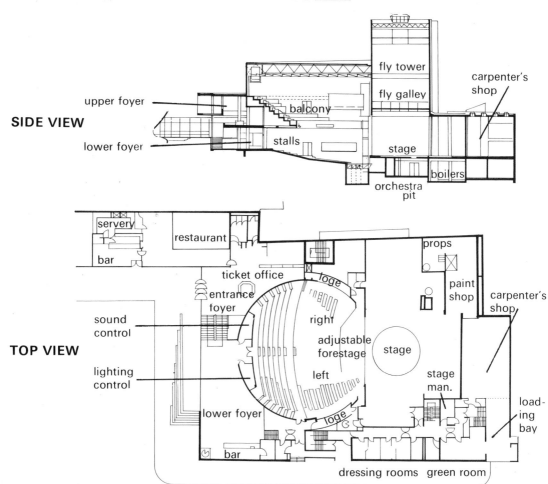

SIDE VIEW

upper foyer

lower foyer

fly tower

fly galley

carpenter's shop

balcony

stalls

stage

boilers

orchestra pit

TOP VIEW

servery

restaurant

bar

props

ticket office

entrance foyer

loge

paint shop

carpenter's shop

sound control

right

adjustable forestage

stage

lighting control

left

stage man.

lower foyer

loge

load-ing bay

bar

dressing rooms   green room

The Orchestra

An orchestra is a group of players who play music together. There are often as many as seventy players in a full orchestra. The instruments which are played can be divided into four groups. The groups are the strings, woodwind, brass and percussion. Each of these groups are divided into sections.

Conductor and Leader

The conductor is the person who guides the orchestra and 'shapes' the music. He uses his hands, or a stick called a baton, to show the speed of the music and if it should be soft or loud. He also makes sure different parts of the orchestra play at the right time.

The leader of the orchestra is the principal first violinist. He is the man the conductor talks to when he is deciding how a piece of music should be played. He sits in front on the conductor's left.

Strings

The strings are the most important group in the orchestra. Two-thirds of the instruments in the orchestra are part of this group. Instruments in this group are violins, violas, cellos and double basses.

Woodwind

The woodwind group has instruments like flutes, clarinets and bassoons. They are mostly wood, but nowadays flutes are often metal. Woodwind instruments are played in different ways. Flute players blow across a hole in the flute. Clarinets have a single reed. Oboes and bassoons have double reeds.

Brass

Brass instruments include trumpets, horns, trombones and tubas. The brass is a very lively part of the orchestra. It is

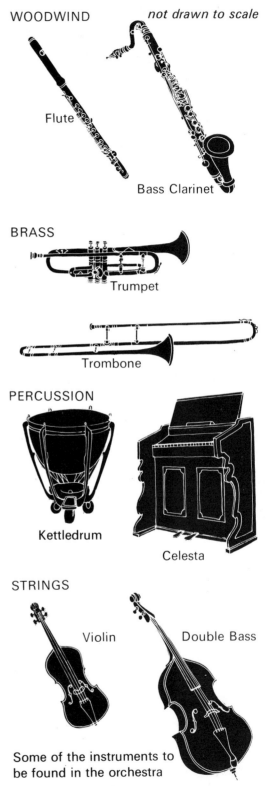

WOODWIND *not drawn to scale*

Flute

Bass Clarinet

BRASS

Trumpet

Trombone

PERCUSSION

Kettledrum

Celesta

STRINGS

Violin

Double Bass

Some of the instruments to be found in the orchestra

often used in pieces of music to make loud and dramatic sounds.

Percussion

Percussion instruments are mostly played by hitting, and make rhythmic sounds. They include triangles, cymbals and different kinds of drums. Some percussion instruments make definite notes, like the celesta. They are called tuned percussion.

What Orchestras play

Orchestras mainly play pieces of music called symphonies and concertos. These are usually in parts called movements. Each movement has a different mood and speed. A symphony is usually just for the orchestra. A concerto has an instrument playing alone and with the orchestra.

In the past composers such as Beethoven often wrote music to celebrate famous people and events. The music had to suit the occasion.

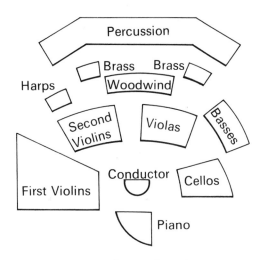

This is a key to show where in an orchestra different kinds of players sit

The Royal Philharmonic Orchestra

Opera

An opera is a play in which people usually sing instead of speaking. Pop songs express all sorts of moods and feelings and so does an opera. But an opera is much longer than a pop song and the music expresses more varied feelings. Opera singers have to have very strong voices or they cannot be heard above the orchestra. Sometimes the part of a young girl is played by an older singer. Her lovely voice makes the audience believe that she is young.

Opera singers need to be strong enough to sing for long periods of time. Some operas are five hours long.

Famous Operas

'Orfeo' was written in 1607 by an Italian called Claudio Monteverdi. It tells the story of Orpheus. His wife is kidnapped by the King of Hell. Orpheus can save her if he leads her out of hell without looking back. But he looks back and loses her forever.

The best operas of the 18th century were by Handel and Mozart. Both spoke German but often composed operas with Italian words. This was because the great singers of their day were all Italians.

'Aida' is a 19th century opera which is still popular today. It was written by Giuseppe Verdi. The opera takes place in Ancient Egypt. It is about an Egyptian soldier and an enslaved Ethiopian princess who fall in love. Their countries are at war. When the soldier refuses to give up his love for the girl Aida, he is condemned to death. He is buried alive in a tomb. He finds Aida hiding in the tomb and they die together.

A famous 19th century composer was

A simple stage set for this Scottish Opera production of Wagners 'The Ring'

A spectacular scene from Giuseppe Verdi's 'Aida'

Richard Wagner. He wrote the famous cycle of operas called 'The Ring'. This is made up of four parts. Each part lasts a whole evening. It begins when an evil dwarf steals some magical gold from the River Rhine. Gods, giants and dragons fight for it, but they are all destroyed and the gold falls back into the river. The story comes from an old German legend.

Opera Today

Modern composers have written works which are easier to put on stage. Some of Benjamin Britten's operas need only eight musicians and are performed in churches. 'Noye's Fludde' is the story of Noah. It uses a cast of children and only two adults. 'Let's Make an Opera' also uses children. The audience sings the chorus parts. They are taught the music during the interval.

The Sydney Opera House in Australia is one of the most exciting new buildings in the world

Ballet

A ballet is a story told in movement with music. A choreographer works out the steps of a dance. He turns the story into movements which fit the music. Ballet began at the court of Louis XIV of France. When young he was a very good dancer. In 1661 he started a school for dancers called 'The Academy'.

High heeled shoes and long heavy skirts made it hard for women to dance. In the 18th century Marie Camargo was famous for her fast leaps and turns. She wore shorter dresses and lower heels.

Great Ballets

In 1832 Filippo Taglioni choreographed 'La Sylphide' for his daughter Marie. The Sylph is a winged spirit. A young Scottish farmer is in love with her. A witch teaches him how to make her into a woman. The Sylph loses her wings but dies at once. Taglioni danced on the tips of her toes to suggest the lightness of the spirit. This is called dancing 'on point'.

'Swan Lake' and 'Sleeping Beauty' have beautiful point dancing. Both these ballets have music by the Russian composer Tchaikovsky.

20th Century Ballet

'Petrouchka' is a Russian ballet about three puppets who come to life. It was first danced in 1911 by Nijinsky. The music is by Stravinsky. Both worked for Diaghilev whose company in the early half of the 20th century produced many great ballets.

Some modern ballets have no point work. Martha Graham is an American choreographer who has become famous for her strong, athletic dancing. Nowadays jazz, rock and electronic music are all used in ballet.

Learning to Dance

Dancers have to train very hard when they are very young. They need to be as strong as football players. At a ballet school they learn how to act with their bodies. They study the music and dances of different countries. They do ordinary school work as well. Few dancers find work in ballet companies. Many dance in stage musicals and television variety shows. They keep fit by doing a dance class every day. Most retire before they are 40.

Right: 'Swan Lake' is a romantic ballet. The girls have been turned into swans

Louis XIV (1638-1715) was proud of his dancing

Marie Camargo (1710-1770) was a great dancer

Marie Taglioni (1804-1884) was the first 'Sylphide'

Nijinsky (1890-1950) is the most famous male dancer

Martha Graham is a very dramatic modern dancer

Eastern Theatre

In Asia there are still many old styles of theatre. The kind of theatre is very different from traditional theatre in the West. The audience has to imagine a great deal of what the actor is trying to say. In this century many Western writers have been influenced by Eastern drama.

Noh Theatre of Japan

Noh theatre began in the 14th century. All the actors wear wooden masks. Different masks are used by the gods, ghosts and ladies in the stories. There are no actresses.

An actor begins to learn the rules at the age of seven. Each movement he makes has an exact meaning. A Noh actor never weeps on stage the way a person does in real life. He holds a hand, palm upwards, under his eyes and bows his head. He makes no noise. But the audience understands that he is crying.

Japanese Kabuki

Kabuki is a much noisier entertainment than Noh. Many of the popular plays are 200 years old. The women's parts all used to be played by men. Now there are a few actresses. Each kind of character has a different colour make-up and style of wig. The scenery often looks very real. A revolving stage makes it easy to change the scenes. When a character is killed in a fight a black cloth is held up to hide him. He drops under the stage on a lift. When the cloth is removed, the body has vanished.

Indian Kathakali

Kathakali dancers act out the stories of well known Indian epic poems. Men with red faces are villains. Men with green faces are heroes. They do not speak. Their

Japanese Noh Theatre. The actors all wear masks. The scenery is very simple and the dance-like movements are accompanied by music

audience imagines what they are saying from their eyes and hand movements.

Chinese Opera

In Chinese opera most of the story is sung. There is a large orchestra. The colour of an actor's make-up shows what kind of part he is playing. Red is for a good man, white for a bad one. There is little scenery. An actor carries an oar to show that he is in a boat. A whip means he is on horseback. The audience has to imagine the boat and the horse. Since 1949 new socialist operas have been written. For the first time women appear. Often they are shown leading the fight against rich landlords and invading armies.

Fierce characters and sword fights are popular in Kabuki plays

Japanese Kabuki Theatre is full of colour and noise. This play is called 'The Double Suicide at Sonezaki'. The lady on the step is played by a male actor

This rich costume is only worn by a princess in Kabuki plays

The Cinema

The first public film shows were in Paris in 1895. They were produced by the Lumière brothers. Each film only lasted a minute. They had no stories. They just showed people walking in the street. Stories were soon written and silent films became the most popular form of entertainment. The first film studio opened in Hollywood, USA, in 1911. Soon it was the world capital of film making. Stars like Mary Pickford, Charlie Chaplin and Douglas Fairbanks all became millionaires and soon were household names around the world.

The Talkies

Until 1927 films were silent. A live orchestra or a piano played in the cinema to set the mood of each scene. In 1927 Al Jolson sang and spoke in 'The Jazz Singer'. The 'talkies' had arrived. Colour films were made as early as 1922, but it was a costly process. Until the 1950's most films were in black and white.

Different Kinds of Films

There are many different kinds of films. There are popular films like westerns, musicals, horror films, comedies and adventure stories.

There are also serious films with stories which could have happened in real life. 'Kes' is about a boy who keeps a kestrel in his back garden. In the end the bird is killed by the boy's elder brother. The film looks at the boy's home and school life. It shows us why the boy liked taking care of the kestrel.

Documentaries are films about real life events. They can be about many different subjects, like the Vietnam War or wildlife in the African jungle. Nowadays more documentaries are shown on television than at the cinema.

Making a Film

To make a popular film you need a good story, stars and a director. 'Gone With the Wind', 'The Godfather' and 'The Sound of Music' are three popular films.

A good director tells stories with pictures, the way a writer does with words. Cameramen and designers help him. After the film has been shot it is edited. Whole scenes are sometimes cut out to make it funnier or more exciting.

Rudolph Valentino

Charlie Chaplin

Mary Pickford

Greta Garbo

Fred Astaire

Humphrey Bogart

Judy Garland

Marilyn Monroe

Marlon Brando

Jack Nicholson

The World Film Industry

Although Hollywood is still the most famous centre for film making, films are now made all over the world.

Thousands of cinemas closed in the late 1950's because of television. People no longer needed to go to the cinema. They could watch television programmes.

The world's first film studio was built in the USA in 1893. Thomas Edison built it in the grounds of his laboratory. It was nicknamed 'The Black Maria' because it looked like a police wagon

Left: The inside of 'The Black Maria' was very simple. The background of the little stage was draped in black cloth. At the other end of the studio was the camera

Below: Many famous people were filmed in the early days of Hollywood

Puppets and Cartoons

Puppet shows are a very old form of entertainment. There were puppets in Egypt 3,000 years ago. Today there are puppet theatres all over the world.

Kinds of Puppets

Marionettes are worked by strings. Most have strings to the head, arms and legs. They have hinges at the neck, elbows, wrists and knees. A good puppeteer can make their movements very life-like. Famous puppet shows such as the Salzburg Marionettes tour all around the world.

Marionettes are moved by strings

Glove Puppets fit over the hand. The first finger moves the head. The thumb and middle finger move the arms. Punch and Judy are glove puppets. Punch stays on the showman's right hand. The other characters appear on the left. Punch is ugly, boastful and rough. But he makes everyone laugh. He has no respect for anyone, not even the hangman. Punch has different names in other countries. In Russia he is Petrushka, in Germany Kaspar, in Italy Pulcinella.

Punch and Judy are the most popular of all glove puppets

Indonesian Shadow Puppets are cut out of very thin leather. They are moved by rods fixed to the head and arms. A strong light throws their shadows onto a screen. Shadow plays are very old and full of dragons, demons and princes.

The idea of making cartoons probably came from shadow plays.

Japanese Bunraku Puppets are half life size. Each is operated by three men. One works the feet, one the left arm and one the right arm and head. They wear black clothes and hoods but are in full view of the audience. Only the leader is bare-headed.

Shadow puppets are found all over Asia. These are from China

Cartoon Films

Cartoons are one of the most popular forms of entertainment.

The most famous cartoon maker is Walt Disney. His 'Mickey Mouse' was first seen in 1928. Cartoons take a long time to make. This is because they are very long and have a lot of action in them. For example Walt Disney spent five years making 'Snow White'.

Making a Cartoon

A cartoon is a series of still pictures. Each picture is a little different from the one before. These pictures are photographed by a film camera. When the film is shown on the screen all the pictures run together so that it looks as if the cartoon character is moving. The drawings on this page show the different stages that go into making a cartoon.

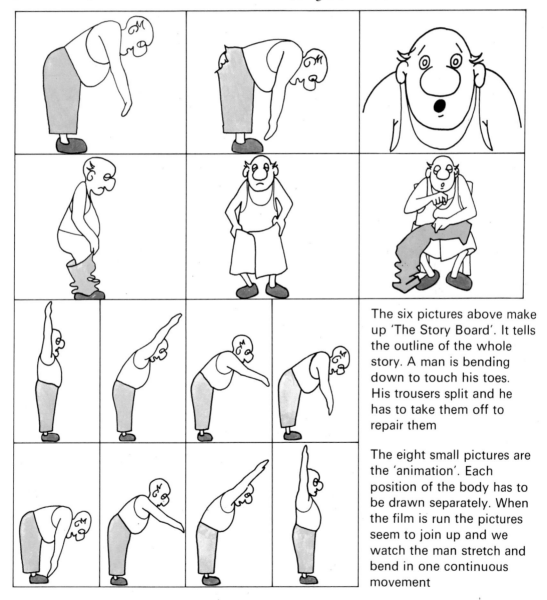

The six pictures above make up 'The Story Board'. It tells the outline of the whole story. A man is bending down to touch his toes. His trousers split and he has to take them off to repair them

The eight small pictures are the 'animation'. Each position of the body has to be drawn separately. When the film is run the pictures seem to join up and we watch the man stretch and bend in one continuous movement

Home Entertainment

A hundred years ago there was no television or radio and no cassette or record players. If people wanted entertainment they had to make it themselves. Many children learned to play a musical instrument. Families often made their own small orchestras. For instance one person played the violin, one the flute and one the harp. When people felt like dancing someone would play a waltz or a polka on the piano. By 1850 more than 300,000 upright pianos were sold each year in the USA alone. These pianists did not play very well, but nobody minded. Few people could afford to go to a concert hall and hear the best musicians.

Songs and Reading Aloud

Almost everybody sang too. The most popular song of the 1890's was a waltz 'After the Ball'. 10 million copies of the piano music were sold. Religious songs were popular with titles like 'The Holy City'. There were also many sad songs. 'Father's a Drunkard and Mother is Dead' was one of many which described the evils of drink.

People also used to recite poetry. 'The Charge of the Light Brigade', by Tennyson, told the story of a brave but foolish charge in the Crimean War. The popular novels of the time were published in monthly instalments. Father would often read aloud to the whole family. 'Oliver Twist' and 'Dombey and Son', both by Charles Dickens, could make listeners laugh and cry.

Home Entertainment Today

When radio and television first became popular people no longer wanted their pianos. Old ones were thrown on the scrap heap and sales of new ones dropped. But in the last twenty years the sale of pianos has risen again. And more people than ever are learning to play. Folk, Skiffle and Rock 'n Roll music started a craze for the guitar in the 1960's. Young people everywhere learned a few simple chords and sang popular songs by The Beatles or Bob Dylan. An acoustic (non-electric) guitar is not loud enough to worry your neighbours. People still make their own entertainment in the age of television and cinema. They find that taking part themselves in music-making or some other hobby is often far more rewarding.

Right: Whole families used to sing and play musical instruments. Musical evenings were a very popular form of entertainment

A girl plays the guitar in her own room. She is probably singing one of the songs recorded by her favourite singer. Amateurs have enjoyed playing the guitar for more than 400 years. The electric guitar has only become popular in the last 20 years

Right: A night out. Most people enjoy getting together with their friends and having a sing-song and a dance. All through history, people have enjoyed themselves in this way

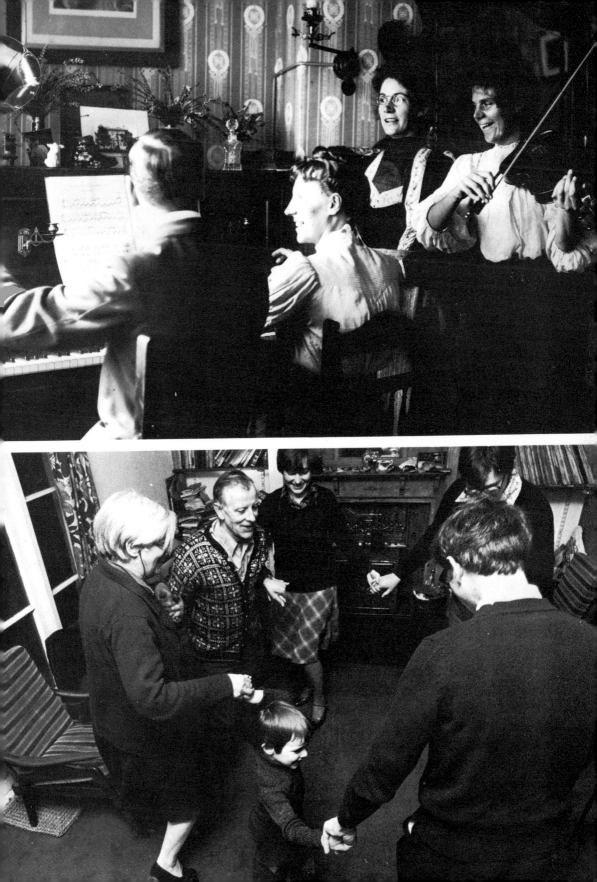

Music from Machines

Nowadays anyone can listen to music whenever they feel like it on records or on radio. But 100 years ago a clockwork musical box was the only machine which could make music in the home. When the motor was wound up it turned a cylinder. Dozens of pins on the cylinder struck fixed metal prongs as it turned. The prongs were tuned to the notes of the musical scale. 'Home Sweet Home' and 'The Last Rose of Summer' were favourite musical box tunes. Each box had only one cylinder. It could only play one or two tunes over and over again.

A clockwork musical box

In the 1890's there was a disc musical box. The discs could be changed and all the popular tunes were available. In cafes and pubs they were worked by dropping a coin into a slot, just like a juke box.

Phonographs and Gramophones

The invention of the phonograph and the gramophone changed the whole nature of the music industry. Records were to become big business.

A cylinder recording machine

Thomas Edison recorded the human voice in 1877. His phonograph played sounds recorded on a cylinder covered in tin foil. In 1888 Emile Berliner made a gramophone with discs played on a turntable. The quality of sound was not good until electrical recording began to be used in the 1920's. Records were played at 78 revolutions per minute (rpm). Each side lasted for five minutes or less. The first long playing records (LP's) were sold in 1948. Narrower grooves and the slower speed of $33\frac{1}{3}$ rpm made it possible to put an hour's music on one disc. From the middle of the 1950's pop singles were recorded at 45 rpm on smaller, tougher

Here is an opera singer making a cylinder recording of her voice. Some recordings from 1900 still exist but they are not very good

discs. This meant that 78's gradually died out. Modern records are usually 'stereophonic' (recorded for playing through two loudspeakers).

The Record Business

Records have been big business for more than 50 years. In 1922 more than 100 million records were sold in the USA. Today most records are made by big international companies. But there are also small companies who only produce special kinds of music such as Reggae or Jazz. Many pop records owe their success to the record producer. He makes the song and group sound as good as possible. Often he hires extra players for the recording session. That is why some groups sound different in live shows than they do on their records.

Most people only buy a record after they have heard it on the radio or at a discotheque. The disc-jockey has become a very important person in making sure records are heard and bought.

A big horn took the place of a loudspeaker in early gramophones

A modern stereo deck for records and tapes

The disc-jockey is one of the main forces in the selling of records

Pop Music

Pop music is the music that is most popular at the time. Fashions in music are always changing. But the pop sounds of the 1970's all began with Rhythm and Blues and Rock 'n Roll in the 1950's. These kinds of beat music were first played by black musicians like Chuck Berry and Fats Domino. But it was a white group, Bill Haley and his Comets, who took up this style of music and shook the world in 1955 with 'Rock Around the Clock'. Elvis Presley also changed his style of singing by listening to black singers. His first million-selling disc was 'Heartbreak Hotel' in 1956 and he soon became the main influence on the pop music of his day.

The Roots of Pop Music

Gospel songs, the Blues and Jazz all began in the southern states of America in the 19th century. They were the songs and dances of black slaves. The blacks brought instruments like banjos and drums with them from Africa. They mixed their own songs and tunes with European hymns and folk tunes. Pop grew out of a mixture of all these sounds. Reggae and Soul are two modern pop sounds created by black musicians. Bob Marley and the Wailers are one West Indian Reggae group who have become very popular internationally.

Elvis Presley has been a top pop star for more than 20 years

The Beatles wrote and sang some of the most popular songs of the 1960's

Bob Marley first became popular in the West Indies but is now heard all round the world

The Stars

There were pop stars before Rock 'n Roll. Frank Sinatra was mobbed by fans even in the 40's. Since then most pop music has been aimed at people below the age of twenty. In the past young people did not have much money. Now they buy most of the records sold.

Some of their favourite stars have taught themselves to play and sing. Others have studied music at college. Many are songwriters as well as singers.

Having an Image

The Beatles sold more records than any group before or since. But it was not just good songs which made them famous, it was their image. In the early 1960's they all had long hair. It was cut in a certain style which became fashionable – the Beatle haircut. They also wore a new style of suit. The jackets had no lapels.

The 'image' which a pop star or pop group invents is very important. It can be taken up and copied by fans Elton John plays music which thousands of people like to hear, but his colourful suits and glittering spectacles make sure that everyone remembers his style.

39

Radio and Television

In Britain the average family watches television for five hours every day. People no longer have to go outside the home for information or entertainment. The most popular serials and comedy shows are seen by more than a quarter of the whole population. A big sporting event has an even larger audience.

Radio is still very popular because it can be listened to while you are doing other things. The largest audiences listen to the popular music programmes.

The Start of Radio

Guglielmo Marconi, an Italian inventor, sent the first radio message across the Atlantic in December 1901. The first regular radio broadcasts began in 1920 from Pittsburgh in the USA.

The British Broadcasting Company (fore-runner of the Corporation) was formed in 1922. It began to broadcast music and talks. People listened in on 'crystal sets'. You could only hear properly through headphones.

The Start of Television

In 1929 John Logie Baird made his first television broadcast from the BBC in London. It was watched on a screen only fifteen by ten centimetres. Regular broadcasts were started by the BBC in 1936. In the USA television began in 1942. By 1974 there were 948 stations. In New York and Los Angeles viewers have a choice of more than seven different channels. Colour television was developed during the 1950's and is now in general use.

How a Play is Made

The outdoor scenes in a television play are filmed first. Then the actors and director rehearse the rest of the play in a

An early broadcast in the USA by NBC. Until the 1950's radio was far more important than television. News broadcasts were listened to by millions

This picture was taken in a plane in 1931. The plane's passengers are listening to the broadcast of a boat race. Radio coverage of sport and music completely changed the world of entertainment

large room. Marks on the floor show what shape the sets will be. Actors have to move exactly so as to be in the right place for the cameras. When they go into a studio, it is full of people in charge of cameras, lights, sound, costumes and make-up. It normally takes two days to record a play. A 'video recorder' puts the pictures and sounds on to tape. Plays are recorded months before they are shown to the public.

Actors rehearsing a television play; at first they read their parts from scripts

Television by Satellite

Television broadcasts from America to Europe began in July 1962. A Telstar satellite was put into orbit 35,000 kilometres above the earth. Satellites make it possible for a thousand million people all over the world to watch a live sporting event, a state occasion, or an important space shot, just as it happens.

The director's gallery in a television studio. He chooses which picture to record or transmit

The floor of a television studio during the recording of a play about Napoleon

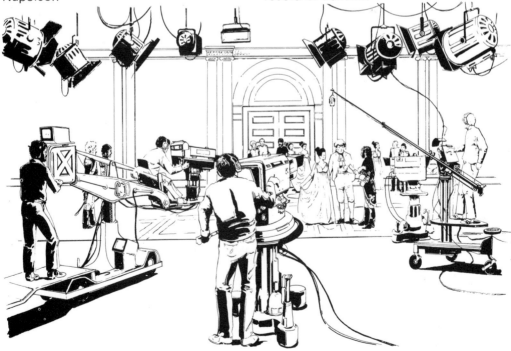

What is Television for?

Most people watch television because they enjoy the different programmes. There are the programmes which are fun to watch. These include the adventure series like 'Star Trek' and 'Starsky and Hutch'. People get to know and like the characters they see every week. Comedy programmes like 'Tom and Jerry' are also very popular.

Television is also a very easy way of finding out what is happening in the world. News programmes and documentaries help people to do this. For example, if there is a war going on in some part of the world a camera crew films it and millions of people see what is actually happening.

Television is also used to educate people. There are programmes which tell people how to do many different things, from learning to cook to mending a house. There are also educational programmes put on especially for schools.

Entertainment and Advertising

In most countries there is a television station owned by the Government. There are also stations run by commercial companies. In Britain the BBC is an independent body set up by the Government. BBC programmes are paid for from licence fees. Everyone with a television set has to buy a licence each year.

The British commercial network is known as ITV. ITV programmes are paid for from advertisements. Advertisers want ITV programmes to be very popular. It costs them up to £6,000 every time one of their advertisements is shown. Their money would be wasted if no one was watching.

The programmes which advertisers like best are popular serials like 'Coronation Street' and 'Crossroads'. These are watched by a huge audience. People turn on their sets at the same time each night to find out what their favourite characters are doing. This gives advertisers a good chance to sell their products.

But television also brings ballet, opera, concerts and circuses into millions of homes. It is the way that most people first find out about all the many exciting kinds of live entertainment.

Right: Animals are used in lots of advertisements because most people love them. Chimps, cats and dogs are often trained to seem very human. The audience laughs at their antics but remembers to buy a particular brand of product next time they are out shopping

'Crossroads' is one of the most popular series. The story is simple and goes on week after week. The audience likes Meg Richardson and always switches on to find out what will happen next to her. So millions see the advertisements in between scenes

Right: This advertisement shows us a happy family in their own home. Everyone is smiling and comfortable. The children are very polite and well behaved. We are meant to believe that a coal fire would make every home as happy as this one

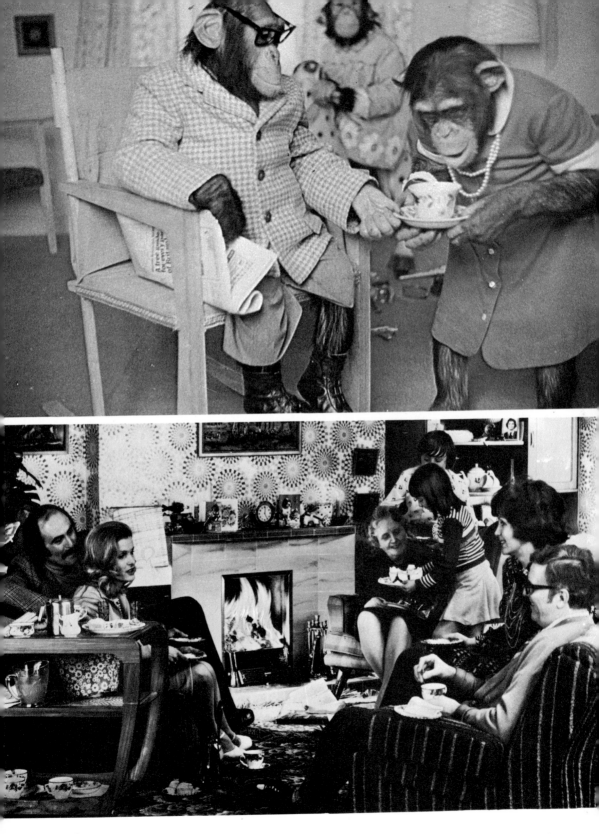

43

Books to Read

Markets and Fairs, Dorner; Wayland 1974

Circuses and Fairs, White, Paul; Black 1972

My Wild Life, Chipperfield; Macmillan 1975

I Scream for Ice Cream, Brandreth (ed.) Eyre Methuen 1974

The Theatre, Macdonald First Library; Macdonald Educational 1974

Theatre through the Ages; Molinari; Cassell 1975

Shakespeare's Theatre, Hodges; OUP 1974

The World of Musical Instruments, Kendall; Hamlyn 1972

A Concise History of Opera, Olley; Thames and Hudson 1972

Ballet for all, Brinson, Crisp; Pan 1970

Story of the Cinema, Fen; Wayland 1974

The Cinema, Macdonald First Library; Macdonald Educational 1974

Punch and Judy, Speaight; Studio Vista 1970

Fun with Puppets and Soft Toys, Janitch; Kaye and Ward 1974

Encyclopedia of Rock, Vols 1, 2, 3, Hardy and Laing (eds.); Granada 1976

The Facts about a Pop Group, Whizzard; Andre Deutsch 1976

Book of Television, Baxter; BBC 1969

Television, King, Blackie 1969

You will find books about all the great writers and performers in every bookshop and library. Not many of them are written especially for young readers, but the life stories of people like Margot Fonteyn and Charles Chaplin are a good way of finding out what it is like to be a great dancer or comedian.

Places to Go

Your local library will have information about the different forms of entertainment that are happening in your town or village. Most theatres put on shows especially for young people.

Well known places of entertainment are:

For Opera and Dance
Royal Opera House
Covent Garden
London WC2
English National Opera
The Coliseum
St Martin's Lane
London WC2
Sadler's Wells Theatre
Rosebery Avenue
London EC1
For Information about the Theatre
Victoria and Albert Museum
Exhibition Road
London SW7
Theatre Museum
Leighton House
Holland Park Road
London W14

Index

Illustrations appear in bold type.